Mantegna

Cover
The Court of the Gonzaga,
detail, ?–1747.
Castle of San Giorgio (Palazzo Ducale),
Camera degli Sposi, Mantua.

Texts by Stefano Zuffi

Translation by Richard Sadleir

Photograph References
Sergio Anelli, Milan
Cameraphoto, Venice
Electa Archives, Milan
Giancarlo Giovetti, Mantua
Photo Service Gruppo Editoriale Fabbri, Milan
Mario Quattrone, Florence
Scala, Florence

This volume was printed by Elemond S.p.a.
at the plant in Martellago (Venice) in 1997

Mantegna

Electa/Art Books International

Mantegna

Andrea Mantegna's life and the development of his art coincided with a period of important changes. The luxurious, courtly Gothic style was being swept away by a profound interest in classical civilization. Men of letters and artists, first in Florence, then in the other ancient university towns and finally in the whole of Italy, were creating the premises for a cultural and civic ideal based on man; this was the age of the humanists. The intellectual and ethical qualities inspired by the study of Greek and Latin literature and philosophy led to the analysis of the harmonious proportions of the human body, as providing an ideal "measure" for architecture and town planning. The Middle Ages had always subordinated worldly affairs to the will of Almighty God; but during the fifteenth century there was a progressive rediscovery of the greatness of man, the maker of his own history.

Artists, helped by a steady proliferation of theoretical studies, were given the responsibility for making this concept visibly present.

Stimulated by this new age of art and thought, Andrea Mantegna became one of its most committed interpreters. His formative years were spent Padua, in the very period when great Tuscan artists were active there. The humanist tradition had deep roots in Padua (the memory of Petrarch's sojourn in the city was still vivid), and in no other city in Northern Italy was such a wealth of new ideas at the centre of debate. From childhood on, Mantegna was enabled to pursue a great ideal with passion and conviction: interpretation of "northern" humanism, sustained by constant cultural commitment and a confident understanding of the classical world.

Mantegna kept this aim steadily before him; and yet his work developed amid an

Self Portrait. Mantua, Castle of San Giorgio, Camera degli Sposi.

immense variety of different currents. His youth was spent in the chaotic but lively *bottega* run by Squarcione, offering him examples of advanced experiments in technique and perspective as well as the dying glow of Venetian goldwork. Later his links with Venice and journeys to Ferrara, Florence and Rome offered him a crescendo of new emotions and a definite framework of ideas.

From the age of thirty until his death Mantegna was the court artist to the Gonzaga in Mantua. Here the cultural situation was very different from in Padua and he brought about innovations in the local decorative tradition in secular art, rejecting Pisanello's knightly visions for a more clearly organized kind of painting, no less rich in invention, in a Renaissance style with a serene yet moving erudition. Mantegna's role in Quattrocento Italy consisted above all in his precocious ability to interpret the most advanced cultural and artistic concepts and apply them in his own original way, not just as a carefully pondered and austere vision of man in the world, but also in festively decorative terms. In this regard, Mantegna's experiments with perspective were of immense importance for the new generation of artists. His fame spread widely and rapidly, and his influence was felt over a large part of Italy and the North, partly through his renowned engravings. It was largely due to Mantegna, in fact, that the Renaissance developed into a fully European movement.

A "Child Prodigy" in Padua (1440–1459)

Andrea Mantegna's adolescence and training as an artist were surprisingly similar to the cliché of the child prodigy. Born late in 1430 or early in 1431 at Isola di Carturo, not far from Piazzola di Brenta, Andrea was the son of a modest carpenter named Biagio. His childhood was poor and ended early, when he was sent to Padua (where an elder brother lived) to enter the *bottega* of Francesco Squarcione, who treated him almost as an adopted son.

Squarcione's extraordinary workshop was like a sample case of the remarkable development of art in mid-fifteenth century Padua. The presence of a glorious university, the love of classical antiquity initiated by Petrarch and maintained by archaeological research, the importance—also in terms of economic power and commissions for paintings—of two important religious centres, the basilica of Saint Antony of Padua and the Benedictine abbey of Santa Giustina, together with the splendid artistic tradition inherited from the previous century (when masters like Giotto, Giovanni Pisano, Giusto de' Menabuoi, Guariento, Altichiero and Avanzo had worked in the city), all made Padua a centre of attraction not only for Venetian and North Italian artists but also for painters and sculptors from Tuscany, who were well to the fore in experiments with perspective.

In the very period when Mantegna was working there as an apprentice, great Florentine masters were active in Padua: Paolo Uccello, Filippo Lippi and above all Donatello, who lived there for over a decade and produced some stupendous bronze sculptures: the high altar for the basilica and the equestrian monument to Gattamelata.

At the same time, the pioneering spirit of the Renaissance artists was counterbalanced by the last, delicate period of Gothic, which appears in the gilding and the rich frames of the polyptyches by Antonio Vivarini and Giovanni d'Alemagna. Padua in the 1440s provided a lively, composite artistic panorama, and the workshop run by Squarcione (not himself a remarkable painter, mentioned in documents rather as a "tailor and embroiderer") reflected in a disorderly and fascinating way all these impulses. Some sources claim that Squarcione had over a hundred pupils: this may well be an exaggeration, but it suggests the size and importance of a workshop which started numerous young artists on important careers—Cosmè Tura, Carlo Crivelli, Marco Zoppo and perhaps also Michael Pacher from Alto Adige. Rejecting the eclecticism of Squarcione's teaching, Mantegna deliberately chose the innovations in perspective and naturalism of the Tuscans. Gifted with a precocious talent, at seventeen he painted an altarpiece (now lost) which showed his substantial independence from Squarcione.

The success of this work was immediate: in 1448 Mantegna was commissioned, together with Nicolò Pizolo, to join the huge team of painters working on the decoration of the Ovetari Chapel in the church of the Eremitani. Events led to Mantegna becoming the principal painter of the frescoes (*Stories of Saint James and Saint Christopher*, Plates 1–3). Despite the serious bomb damage to these frescoes in the Second World War, they still clearly reveal a rigorous feeling for antiquity, expressed through severe, monumental forms and accurate presentation of Latin inscriptions.

Meanwhile Mantegna broadened his cultural horizons. A journey to Ferrara brought him into contact with circles open to Flemish influences (especially that of Roger van der Weyden) and the monumentality of Piero della Francesca. He also formed bonds with the Bellini family: he knew the album of drawings collected by Jacopo, followed the progress of Giovanni, who was the same age as himself, and in 1451 he married Nicolosia, the daughter of Jacopo Bellini and

Attributed to Andrea Mantegna, *The Descent to Limbo*. Princeton, Barbara Piasecka Collection.

Circle of Andrea Mantegna, *Triumphs of Caesar. The Elephants*. Private Collection.

sister of Giovanni and Gentile Bellini. An interesting point of camparison between the two painters is Mantegna's *Agony in the Garden* in the National Gallery, London (Plate 6).

These experiences soon found their way into a new and important polyptych for the chapel of St. Luke (Plate 4), painted for the abbey of Santa Giustina and now in the Brera Gallery in Milan. This, though still painted with the gold-ground technique, has a definite perspective structure, while the *Saint Euphemia* in the Capodimonte Gallery in Naples (Plate 5) recalls the noble grandeur of Donatello's statues for the bronze altar of the basilica of Sant'Antonio.

In 1457 Mantegna was given an extremely important commission for an altarpiece for the balisica of San Zeno in Verona, which delayed his arrival at Mantua. The *Polyptych of San Zeno* (Plates 8, 9) is one of Mantegna's most complex works and concludes the youthful phase of his art. The original frame is the organic completion of the painting's grand architectural structure, based on a broad, solemn perspective. The austere composition of the *Sacra Conversazione* in the three main panels is barely softened by the rich swags of fruit and foliage festooning the upper part, while in the cragged scenes of Christ's Passion represented in the predella it takes on harshly epic tones. (The predella is now distributed between the Louvre and the museum of Tours).

Having completed the *Polyptych of San Zeno*, and after painting the refined *Saint Sebastian* now in the Vienna Kunsthistorisches Museum (Plate 7), characterized by classical and archaeological features as well as a rugged, dramatic natural landscape, Mantegna finally accepted the generous and insistent invitations of the *marchese* Ludovico Gonzaga to accept the post of court painter in Mantua.

The Camera degli Sposi: A Period of Journeys for Study and Early Success in Mantua (1460–1490)

In 1460 Mantua was hardly comparable to Padua as an artistic centre: it lacked great masters to serve as models, patronage was limited to the Gonzaga court, the humanist cultural renewal was barely beginning, and the artistic tradition was still under the influence of Pisanello's courtly Gothic scenes. The persistence of this tradition helps to explain the themes and style adopted by Mantegna in his first decade in Mantua. In addition to the kind of work typical of a court painter (decorations for furnishings, cartoons for tapestries, curious drawings and other kinds of ornamental work) he painted portraits of the members of the court, produced small paintings and frescoes for a chapel in the castle of San Giorgio, now lost, and other decorations for the suburban residences of his patrons (at Marmirolo and Gonzaga).

In the 1460s Mantegna worked on drawings of various motifs, which he later used for engravings (such as the *Descent of Christ into Limbo*) and painted a series of panels of limited size, now divided up among various museums but probably originally connected. Three of them form the so-called "Uffizi Triptych," in which the *Adoration of the Magi* (Plates 10–13) stands out for its rugged landscape. Despite their reduced dimensions, Mantegna's figures retain a classical "gravitas," as shown by the *Death of the Virgin*, now in the Prado (Plates 14, 15), in which the background is a view based on the lakes formed by the Mincio near Mantua. In 1465 work began on the layout of a room in the castle of San Giorgio, destined to be painted by Mantegna. While preparations were being made, the painter felt impelled to verify the progress of his style by examining the state of art in

Central Italy, and between 1466 and 1467 visited Florence and Pisa. Of particular importance to him was his study of the chapel frescoed by Benozzo Gozzoli in the Palazzo Medici in Florence, for its attractive narrative rhythms and the presence of figures of large dimensions. Probably in about 1471, Andrea Mantegna began the decoration of the *Camera degli Sposi* (Plates 21–26), which became a model for secular painting in the Renaissance. In it he rejected the preciosity and minutiae of courtly Gothic for scenes with a robust sense of perspective and accurate natural observation. Along the main walls two scenes are presented: the "group portrait" of the family of the *marchese* Ludovico II Gonzaga, surrounded by courtiers, and the meeting between Ludovico and his second-born son, the Cardinal Francesco Gonzaga. In the vault, in the middle, of the coffered ceiling, decorated with grisaille classical motifs, there is the famous circular opening representing a balcony with a number of figures and animals leaning over the parapet, creating a giddy perspective view open to the sky. This *trompe l'œil* scene became a model for artists in the generations to come, in particular for Correggio.

The *Camera degli Sposi* was probably completed in 1474. The following decade was a very unhappy one for Mantegna and the state of Mantua. The artist, who had long been engaged in a frequent exchange of letters with the Gonzaga family—his correspondence reveals Mantegna's difficult character and his often troubled relations with the other members of the court—lost his own son, soon followed by the deaths of the *marchese* Ludovico, the *marchesa* Barbara, and then of Federico, Ludovico's successor. It was only with the installation of Francesco II Gonzaga (in 1484) that there was an effective return to the policy of commissioning

works of art. In the meantime Mantegna continued to refine his taste for classical antiquity: he supervised construction of his own house, notable for its circular court, in the San Sebastiano area; he began a collection of Roman marbles (praised by Lorenzo il Magnifico, who visited Mantua in 1483), and painted architectural and ornamental fragments in his intense *Saint Sebastian*, now in the Louvre (Plate 27). It is easy to imagine the enthusiasm with which the painter accepted a commission to execute a series of great tempera paintings of the *Triumphs of Caesar*, in which his feeling for the antique embodied itself fully. Soon after undertaking this work, in 1489, Mantegna finally travelled to Rome, where he was the guest of Innocent VIII. During his stay, which was prolonged into 1490, Mantegna painted a chapel (later destroyed) in the Vatican Palace, visited the celebrated hostage Gem, the exotic brother of the Turkish sultan, and carefully studied the monuments of antiquity: nevertheless, his overall reaction was one of disappointment. On returning to Mantua he preferred a literary and somewhat bitter image of antiquity to what he had seen in Rome.

The Classicism of the Last Years and Relations with Isabella d'Este (1490–1506)

On his return to Mantua, Mantegna formed close ties with the new *marchesa*, the cultivated and intelligent Isabella d'Este. Beginning with the *Christ on the Sarcophagus*, now in the Copenhagen museum (Plate 30) and the *Madonna of the Caves* in the Uffizi (Plates 28, 29), he worked out the last phase of his coherent exploration of classical expression: the human figure, austere and rigorous, highly idealized, is made to stand out sharply against the landscape through the energetic handling of line, clearly apparent also in his drawings and engravings. To enhance this approach, Mantegna worked out a technique all his own by painting works in which colour is reduced to the barest essential, achieving the effect of classical bas-reliefs against a marbled background or else monochrome works with cautious gilt highlighting.

The perfect example of this technique is the series of the *Triumphs of Caesar*, now in the royal palace at Hampton Court: it consists of nine canvases showing Caesar's triumphal procession. Vasari considered this Mantegna's true masterpiece ("the best thing he ever produced"), while the Mantuan man of letters Teofilo Folengo held that it represented "the perfect art of the ancient painters." The compositions were repeatedly copied and imitated in the following centuries, as were many other works from Mantegna's late period. This technique was also used for a number of biblical scenes (such as the *Judith* in Dublin, Plate 32, the *Judgement of Solomon* in the Louvre, and the *Samson and Delilah* in the National Gallery, London): they are virtually monochrome compositions, typical of Mantegna's work in the 1490s. Two tempera paintings on canvas have affinities with this series, and are among his most famous works: the *Saint Sebastian* in the Galleria Franchetti at Ca' d'Oro in Venice (Plate 31), and the *Dead Christ* in the Brera Gallery, Milan (Plate 38). Its date uncertain, the *Dead Christ* can be identified with the "*Christo in scurto*" ("foreshortened view of Christ") annotated in the inventory made by his son after Mantegna's death. It is likely that the famous work was painted for his own funerary chapel in the church of Sant'Andrea in Mantua, decorated partly with works by his pupils (including the young Correggio) and a bronze *Self Portrait* which is perhaps the most important example of his far from negligible work as a sculptor.

In the mid-1490s, when Mantua was enriched with the advanced and exquisite taste of Isabella d'Este, Andrea Mantegna worked on his last works of outstanding importance: two altarpieces and the plan of decoration of Isabella's private studio. The *Madonna della Vittoria* (Plates 34, 35), now in the Louvre—was commissioned to celebrate the illusory victory of Francesco Gonzaga against the French under Charles VIII in the battle of Fornovo in 1495. The group of figures clustered around the throne of the Virgin are surrounded by a highly original architecture of plants, a green apse rich in flowers and fruits, with an immense branch of coral hanging in the middle. Equally grand in structure is the *Sacra Conversazione* or *Trivulzio Madonna*, painted in 1497 for the church of Santa Maria in Organo, Verona, now in the Pinacoteca of Castello Sforzesco, Milan (Plate 33).

Meanwhile, Isabella d'Este, with important help from the court poet and man of letters Paride Ceresara, arranged for a private suite, above all a studio for herself, to be laid out in the Palazzo Ducale in Mantua. For it she chose a classical scheme of decoration, with motifs from Greek myth (the paintings from the studio, dismantled in 1605, are now in the Louvre). The commission to translate Ceresara's iconographic scheme into images fell, naturally, to Mantegna in the first instance, who began work with great enthusiasm in 1497.

While Mantegna's brother-in-law, Giovanni Bellini, in Venice, was engaged in achieving a breakthrough in light and tone which was to determine the course of Venetian painting all through the Cinquecento, and Leonardo in Milan was carefully studying how to reproduce natural features and atmospheric effects in

Virgin and Child. Vienna, Graphische
Sammlung Albertina.

painting (Leonardo was himself a guest of the Gonzagas in the year 1500), Mantegna never abandoned an essentially graphic, incisive manner, rich in ornamental detail and delicate landscapes. It was a techinque that was almost beginning to have an air of nostalgia about it, and yet it sustained the master in his last masterpieces, which might be taken as a symbol of the conclusive phase of humanism in the Italian courts. The painting of *Parnassus* (Plate 36) centres on the elegant dance of the Muses, to the sound of Apollo's lyre, while all around the images of Vulcan, Mars, Venus, Cupid, Mercury and the winged horse Pegasus reveal Mantegna's full acceptance of a mythical and impossible world, which is also suggested in the extravagant forms of the rocks and mountains. Even more unpredictable is the work that followed this, executed in 1504, the painting of *Pallas Expelling the Vices from the Garden of the Virtue* (Plate 37), dominated by the energetic and dynamic figure of the goddess in the act of ousting a host of monsters, symbolizing the vices, from a garden peopled with mysterious presences, while even the clouds in the sky seem to take on human form.

Early in 1506 Mantegna suffered from a deterioration in his health, while money anxieties were also pressing, for he decided to sell the most precious piece in his archaeological collection to Isabella d'Este: a bust of Faustina still in the Palazzo Ducale in Mantua. Meanwhile he began work on a third painting for the studio— *The Fable of the God Comus*—but his death on 13 September of the same year prevented him from completing it.

The Legacy

Mantegna's style, even in his last works, is substantially bound up with Quattrocento concerns and techniques. Even Lorenzo Costa, a painter from Ferrara who followed him as court painter to the Gonzagas in 1507 (for whom he completed the *Fable of Comus*), showed more interest in atmospheric effects in painting.

Yet Mantegna's art is of decisive importance, and not just because of its pioneering character, as the first and most important sign of the spread of artistic humanism in Northern Italy and especially in the Veneto through the work of his brother-in-law Giovanni Bellini.

Leonardo himself, despite his opposition of a vibrant naturalistic analysis to Mantegna's ideal classicism, admired and imitated the decorations with swags of fruit and flowers which were typical of Mantegna's work. Echoes appear in the vaulting of the Sala delle Asse in the Castello Sforzesco in Milan and the lunettes over the *Last Supper*.

Even more directly influenced was Correggio, who had been Mantegna's pupil and collaborator in Mantua. Influenced by Mantegna's studies of illusionistic space, above all in the Camera degli Sposi, with its *trompe l'œil* opening to the sky, Correggio found inspiration to embark on ever more daring perspective schemes, culminating in the cupola of Parma cathedral.

The Renaissance artist who recalls Mantegna most closely is Dürer, who made two journeys to Italy. The German artist took over certain motifs from Mantegna, above all the precise and incisive character of his landscapes, and the use of archaeological features. For Dürer, too, the study of perspective and the proportions of the human body were a passion.

After the first two decades of the Cinquecento, however, admiration for Mantegna began to decline. In Mantua, where many men of letters and coutiers still mourned for Andrea, it was the age of Giulio Romano, who favoured a type of secular decoration that was very different from his predecessor's, while the *morbidezza* inherited from Raphael made Mantegna's manner seem even harsher and "dryer." So while Vasari, in his *Lives*, praises him on the whole, he also systematically associates his work with a certain "hardness."

It was only towards the end of the seventeenth century that the *abbé* Luigi Lanzi sought, without much success, to destroy this cliché. In the second half of the nineteenth century, however, many artists chose Mantegna as their model, including Impressionists like Manet, Degas and Van Gogh.

Critical studies began to proliferate (Berenson, Cavalcaselle, Crowe) and there were numbers of monographs devoted to his work, among which the researches of Kristeller and Fiocco were of outstanding importance. Roberto Longhi has the merit of having reconstructed the cultural environment in Padua in the years around 1450 and also in Squarcione's *bottega*, so revealing the complex influences that were at work on Mantegna as a young artist.

The destruction of the Ovetari Chapel (the most serious loss suffered by Italian art in the last war, save for the demolition of Montecassino) was a bitter blow, and from the fifties on Mantegna has been one of the most widely admired of all artists. His popularity was boosted by a great, evocative exhibition held in the Palazzo Ducale, Mantua, in 1961.

Over the last thirty years studies have mostly focused on the specific theme of Mantegna's use of perspective. In 1986 R. Lightbown published the latest, monumental biography of the artist, which, however, leaves undecided a critical point of some importance, namely the relationship between painting, drawing and engraving in Mantegna's work.

Four Figures Dancing. Boston, Museum of Fine Arts.

Bronze bust of Andrea Mantegna. Mantua, church of Sant'Andrea.

Where to See Mantegna's Works

A fair number of Mantegna's paintings—about a hundred— have survived, but this is not a large number in comparison to his long working life which covered over fifty years, stretching from the mid-fifteenth century to the first decade of the sixteenth. Two contrasting facts have to be borne in mind: Mantegna also worked as a draughtsman and engraver and perhaps as a sculptor and architect, extending his creativity well beyond the sphere of painting; at the same time many important works have been lost, especially frescoes. A number of portraits and whole decorative cycles have been destroyed, like those for the Gonzaga residences at Marmirolo, Cavriana, Goito and Gonzaga, as well as the chapel of the castle of San Giorgio in Mantua. Particularly serious is the loss of the decoration of the chapel of Pope Innocent VIII in the Vatican. Finally the remains of the frescoes in the Ovetari Chapel still produce a painful impression; despite its almost total destruction by bombing raids in World War Two, the remains are still essential to an understanding of Mantegna's astonishing debut as an artist and increase our regret for all that has been lost.

However, this list of losses should not create the impression that it is difficult to undertand his development: on the contrary, the shape of his career is sufficiently clear and one can follow his path as an artist through all the phases of his life's work. Driven to experiment with new forms of art in competition with the artists of antiquity, Mantegna substantially enlarged the range of expressive techniques. While nearly all fifteenth-century artists limited their work mostly to fresco or tempera on panels, Mantegna frequently used canvas, even for large works, and experimented with miniatures, cartoons for tapestries and designs for goldsmith's work. Moreover, using painting for trompe l'œil effects, he often painted false bas-reliefs and monochrome works: first among the Italian masters he understood the opportunities offered by engraving, not only as a way of fostering the spread of pictorial models but also (and above all) as an independent art open to further invention and exploration. Adding to these techniques his experience as a sculptor in terracotta and bronze, Mantegna was able to create a synthesis between the different forms of expression, and in his finest works he achieved a remarkable syncreticism.

If one reflects on these qualities, one comes to see a very different Mantegna. One's initial impression of rigidity and an obstinate adhesion to an idea of the classical Renaissance gradually change into an understanding of an artist whose art developed constantly, through experiment and the quest for innovation. This view of the artist emerged spendidly from the great exhibition held in spring 1992 at the Royal Academy of Arts in London, with the *Triumphs of Caesar* as its centrepiece, after long and careful restoration. This exhibition was a landmark in the critical understanding of Mantegna, especially in its exploration of the relationship between the different techniques he used. As a court painter, Mantegna often turned his hand to profane and literary subjects. Here, too, his experience was

---

exceptional. Though the renewal of the traditional imagery of religious scenes engaged much of his energy, he also produced unprecendented images, tackling complex subjects and giving visible form to complicated poetical, allegorical and economiastic themes.

Mantegna's works are now widely scattered, and this is all the more remarkable when one thinks that originally they were all contained within an area of a few dozen square miles, between Padua, Verona and Mantua. Their present distribution has left only a third of his works in Italy (nearly all the most important ones), while the rest are mostly in Britain, the United States and the Louvre.

Works in Italy

The quest for Mantegna's works in Italy naturally begins with the places where they still exist in their original settings and then takes us as far afield as Naples in search of works in museums.

Padua

The Ovetari Chapel in the church of the Eremitani contains part of the frescoes painted by the youthful Mantegna on *Stories from the Life of Saint Cristopher* and *Saint Lawrence* and the monumental *Assumption* behind the altar: unfortunately they are only the fragments of a cycle largely destroyed by the bombing.

In the Museo Antoniano, annexed to the Basilica of Sant'Antonio, there is also a lunette with *Saint Antony* and *Saint Bernardino*, originally over the sanctuary portal.

Verona

The high altar of the the Basilica of San Zeno still has the wonderful *Triptych* in its original frame. The three panels of the predella are copies of the originals, carried off to France in the Napoleonic period.

The Museum of Castelvecchio has a fine *Holy Family* as well as two other canvases whose attribution is uncertain.

Mantua

The dispersal of the collection of the Gonzagas and the destruction of their country residences has led to the almost total loss of the many pictures Mantegna painted in forty years as court painter. The Palazzo Ducale (more precisely the Castle of San Giorgio) still contains the *Camera degli Sposi*, an epitome of Mantegna's art and a landmark for the whole of Renaissance Italy.

In the church of Sant'Andrea there remain some traces of the the tondi painted on the facade and above all the intact *Mantegna Chapel*, with decorations from the master's workshop (where the young Correggio was one of the artists), and the tomb, adorned with a bronze bust which may be the work of Mantegna himself.

Finally it is important to remember the *House of Mantegna*, a building believed to have been designed by the artist and distinguished by its unusual circular courtyard.

Venice

Museums in Venice contain two very important works, as well as some of uncertain attribution. The Gallerie delle Accademia possess a refined *Saint George* while the Galleria Franchetti in Ca' d'Oro contains a large, dramatic *Saint Sebastian*.

Milan

This city probably has the richest collection of Mantegnas in its museums. The Pinacoteca di Brera has celebrated works like the powerful *Dead Christ*, the *Polyptych of Saint Justine* and the *Madonna of the Cherubim*; also interesting is the attribution to Mantegna of the *Saint Bernardino*.

No less important than the works in Brera is the altarpiece with a *Sacra Conversazione* at the Pinacoteca Civica in the Sforza castle, from the church of Santa Maria in Organo, Verona. Finally, there are two small works: a delicate *Madonna Child* and a *Portrait of a Man*.

Florence

The Uffizi gallery has a rich selection of paintings by Mantegna: a group from the central phase of his output, some of them originally part of a single work, the so-called "Triptych," comprising the *Circumcision*, the *Ascension*, the *Madonna of the Caves* and the *Portrait of Cardinal Carlo de' Medici*.

Naples

The solemn figure of *Saint Euphemia*, a precious example of Mantegna's early work, is in the Gallerie di Capodimonte together with a refined *Portrait of a Prelate of the House of Gonzaga*.

Other Locations in Italy

Other important works by Mantegna in Italy are the *Madonna and Child* in the Accademia Carrara in Bergamo, the *Sacra Conversazione* in Turin's Galleria Sabauda, the fragment of *Christ with the Soul of the Virgin* in the Pinacoteca Nazionale in Ferrara and the ascetic Christ at *Correggio (Reggio Emilia)*.

Works Outside Italy

There are three main groups of works by Mantegna outside Italy: in Paris, London and Berlin. But their distribution is heavily weighted in favour of English-speaking countries (Britain, Ireland and the United States).

Paris

Mantegna's works in the Louvre are essential to an understanding of the painter. Of outstanding interest are the monumental and dramatic *Saint Sebastian of Aigueperse*, the brilliant *Madonna della Vittoria* and above all the two compositions originally painted for the study of Isabella d'Este, *Parnassus* and *Pallas Expelling the Vices from the Garden of the Virtue*.

The Louvre also has one of the panels of the San Zeno triptych; the other two are in the museum of *Tours*.

Also in Paris is the harsh *Ecce Homo* at the Musée Jacquemart-André.

Berlin and Germany

A refined selection of works is contained in the Staatliche Museen in Berlin: the *Madonna and Child with Angels Bearing Instruments of the Passion*, the vigorous *Portrait of Cardinal Mezzarota*, the admirable *Presentation at the Temple* and the initmate, delicate *Madonna and Child*.

London and the British Isles

London's National Gallery has an outstanding collection of Mantegnas. A remarkable piece is the *Agony in the Garden*, while the numerous works painted to simulate marble bas-reliefs are of outstanding interest. Also important is the altarpiece of the *Madonna between Saint John the Baptist and Mary Magdalen*.

The remarkable series of large paintings of *The Triumphs of Caesar* is housed in a special pavilion in the royal castle of Hampton Court.

Another very fine work is the monochrome *Judith and Holofernes* in Dublin's National Gallery of Ireland.

Other European Cities

There are at least three masterpieces in other European museums: the dramatic, bitter image of *Christ on the Sepulchre* in the Statens Museum in Copenhagen; the refined *Saint Sebastian*, with Mantegna's signature in Greek characters, in the Kunsthistorisches Museum in Vienna; and the *Death of the Virigin*, a work of remarkable clarity, in the Prado, Madrid.

United States

American museums have a rich series of Mantegnas, though in some cases the attribution may be uncertain. The most substantial holdings are in *New York*, with the youthful *Adoration of the Shepherds*, the so-called *Butler Madonna*, and a late *Holy Family*. Washington's National Gallery has the *Christ Child* and a very fine *Judith*. The Cincinnati Museum has a noteworthy monochrome painting of *Tarquin and the Sybil*.

1

1–3. Stories of Saint James and Saint Christopher, The Martyrdom and Removal of the Body of Saint Christopher, 1448–?. Church of the Eremitani, Padua. The Ovetari Chapel, in the main apse of the Francescan church, was almost completely destroyed by bombing in 1944. The frescoes were executed by Mantegna and other artists from 1448 on; old black and white photos exist to document their state before destruction. The scenes still visible, here illustrated, reveal the interest shown by Mantegna (who began work on the decoration of the Ovetari Chapel at the age of only seventeen) in the representation of space and the figurative world of antiquity. In the Martyrdom of Saint Christopher, the building in the centre is surrounded by a pergola in perspective, with a number of Roman memorial stones walled into its plinth. From his very earliest work, Mantegna displayed his full acceptance of the cultural and artistic currents of humanism, to which the University of Padua was then making an important contribution.

2

4. Polyptych of Saint Luke, Saint Luke, *1453–1454,* *tempera on panel 119 × 61 cm.* *Pinacoteca di Brera, Milan.* *Executed for the Benedictine monks of the rich and powerful abbey of Santa Giustina in Padua, the polyptych is complete (and has recently been cleaned), but the original frame has been lost. Though it still has a gold ground, the individual figures stand out with monumental force from the surrounding space. The main figure, that of the apostle Luke, is exemplary. He is shown as intent on writing his gospel, resting on a circular table in a highly effective perspective view.*

5. Saint Euphemia, *1454,*
tempera on canvas,
174 × 79 cm. Gallerie
di Capodimonte, Naples.
Imposing and solemn, this work
is coeval with the Polyptych
of Saint Luke. *The tempera*
colours are unfortunately
somewhat darkened, but the
painting is still of immense
interest in understanding the
sculptural fulness of
Mantegna's early works, closely
related as they are to the bronze
statues executed shortly before
by Donatello for the high altar
of Sant'Antonio in Padua.

6

6. The Agony in the Garden,
*1455, tempera on panel,
63 × 80 cm. National Gallery,
London.
This is Mantegna's first famous
landscape: a harsh, craggy
setting rendered with incisive
strokes, which is also evident
in the handling of the figures.
All the features of the scene,
including the clouds, acquire
a hard, almost mineral texture.
The painting is closely related
to a similar composition by his
brother-in-law, Giovanni
Bellini.*

7. Saint Sebastian, *c. 1459,*
tempera on panel, 68 × 30 cm.
Kunsthistorisches Museum,
Vienna.
Mantegna's classicism is wholly
enclosed in this small work,
signed in humanist style in
Greek. With an almost nostalgic
longing for the classical world,
Mantegna dwells on the clarity
of the surfaces, the precision
with which "archaeological"
details are reproduced, and
the careful elegance of the pose
of the martyr.

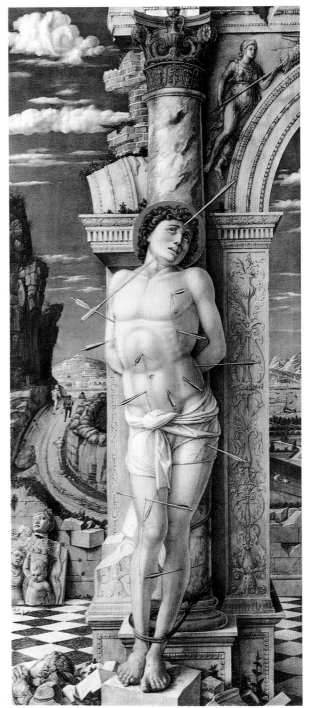

7

9

8, 9. Polyptych of San Zeno, 1457–1459, tempera on panel. Church of San Zeno, Verona. (Central panels with the Madonna Enthroned between Angels and Saints; predella: The Agony in the Garden and the Resurrection, in Tours, Musée des Beaux-Arts; Crucifixion, in the Louvre.)
Though the three panels of the predella are now in French museums, while the triptych in Verona has been supplemented with copies, the work appears as a complete whole, mainly due to the preservation of the frame and the fact that it is still kept in its original setting. This work brings to a close the artist's early period and at the same time opens up the work of his maturity. Certain features, such as the rich festoons of fruit, are typical ornamental motifs of Francesco Squarcione's bottega, while the overall structure of the main scene is wholly new. The frame seems to suggest the divisions of a triptych, but actually the three panels of the main order form a single architectural space divided by pilasters. In the vast space so created the figures are grouped symmetrically. The scenes in the predella, in their turn, evoke a broad definition of space. The Crucifixion in particular, through the landscape of bare, splintered rock, possesses a harsh expressive force, enhanced by the accuracy of the handling of detail.

10

10–13. "Triptych of the Uffizi," 1460–1470, tempera on panel. Uffizi, Florence. Three panels, similar in size, painted with the Resurrection, *the* Adoration of the Magi *and the* Circumcision, *datable to the Mantegna's first years in Mantua and now in the Uffizi Gallery, Florence. They have been inappropriately enclosed in a nineteenth-century frame to form a pseudo-triptych. In reality they were originally a sequence of scenes depicting the life of Christ. Elegant and refined, as appears clearly in the details, they were among the first of Mantegna's works to be enlivened by a narrative structure.*
In the Adoration of the Magi *there is an exceptionally interesting use of landscape, as always harsh and rugged, while the* Circumcision *is set in a rich architectural interior.*

15

14, 15. Death of the Virgin,
1461, tempera on panel,
54 × 42 cm. Prado, Madrid.
This was probably part of the
same sequence which included
the "Triptych of the Uffizi."
The upper section of the
painting, with the tops of the
arches of the ceiling and Christ
bearing away the Madonna's
soul, has been removed and part
of it is kept in the Pinacoteca
Nazionale in Ferrara. The
background of the scene is
renowned: it shows the lakes
formed by the Mincio around
the city of Mantua. The scene
corresponds to the actual view
from a window of the Gonzaga's
Palazzo Ducale.

16

16. The Presentation at the
Temple, *1465–1466, tempera
on canvas, 67 × 86 cm.
Staatliche Museen, Berlin.
Together with panels with small
figures, Mantegna, in his early
years in Mantua, painted a
number of sacred scenes with
groups of half-length figures.
This characteristic arrangement
was widely imitated by
Mantegna's pupils and
followers.*

17–19. Saint George, *1467,*
tempera on canvas,
66 × 32 cm. Gallerie
dell'Accademia, Venice.

17

20

20. Madonna and Child,
1470, tempera on canvas,
43 × 35 cm.
Museo Poldi Pezzoli, Milan.

21

**21–26. Camera degli Sposi,
? – 1474, fresco.
Castle of San Giorgio
(Palazzo Ducale), Mantua.**
The precise chronology of the
execution of these frescoes is not
known. They took some years to
paint and were completed in
1474. Mantegna here reached
the fullest expression of his
mature powers as an artist. He
conceived the room, called the
"Camera Picta" or "Painted
Chamber" in ancient records, as
a unified whole: two sides are
covered with rich drapery, which
opens up on the other walls
on which the members of the
Gonzaga family appear. The
entrance has a wall divided up
by painted pillars covered with
classical motifs and a landscape
rich in allusions to Roman
monuments. This contains the
Meeting between the
Marchese Ludovico Gonzaga
and His Son, with a sumptuous
entourage of pages, caparisoned
horses and pedigree dogs. On
the next wall there follows
The Court of the Gonzaga,
in which Mantegna reveals his
outstanding powers as a
portraitist, varying his technique
to reproduce the fresh cheeks
of the maidens, the severe faces
of their elders and the smile
of the dwarf.
The whole is surmounted by
a circular aperture at the top
of the vault and a trompe l'œil
circular parapet with figures
gazing down in giddy
perspective. The rest of the
ceiling simulates a partition in
decorative stucco plaster panels
with busts of the Roman
emperors.

26

27. Saint Sebastian, *1480*,
tempera on canvas,
275 × 142 cm. Louvre, Paris.
In this dramatic interpretation
of the subject, Mantegna
combines a strong expressive
force and his taste for antiquity.
The column, the sculpture and
ornamental fragments, the
architecture in the background
all form a refined repertory
of archaeological motives.

28

28, 29. Madonna of the
Caves, *1489–1490, tempera
on panel, 29 × 21.5 cm.
Galleria degli Uffizi, Florence.
The painter's sensitive response
to rugged, splintered landscapes
finds an unusual application in
this small masterpiece. On the
pebble-strewn ground, the
Madonna herself seems to share
in the stony substance of the hill
in the background.*

30. Christ on the
Sarcophagus, Supported
by Two Angels, *1490,
panel, 83 × 51 cm.
Statens Museum for Kunst,
Copenhagen.
This noble, intense work was
executed by Mantegna on his
return from Rome, which had
disappointed his expectations
of finding the ancient city he
had long dreamt of. This
classical theme is thus presented
with lucid nostalgia, with
enamelled colours and clear
draughtsmanship, in the very
period when Leonardo and
Giovanni Bellini were
experimenting with softer, more
delicate tones to represent
atmospheric qualities.*

31. Saint Sebastian, *1490,
tempera on canvas,
210 × 91 cm. Galleria
Franchetti at Ca' d'Oro, Venice.
From the dark, neutral
background emerges the
powerful figure of the saint,
the outlines sculpted as if
in statuary. This is another
interpretation of the theme of
Saint Sebastian, frequently dealt
with by Mantegna, who lived
near the church dedicated
to the saint in Mantua.*

31

32

32. Judith with the Head of Holofernes, *1490, canvas, 64 × 30 cm. National Gallery of Ireland, Dublin.*
Painted in a refined and original style, the scene is taken from a bas-relief originally executed on a grainy and slightly-colored marble slab, maintaining the monochrome graphic images of its characters.

33. The Trivulzio Madonna, *1497, tempera on canvas, 287 × 214 cm. Civiche Raccolte d'Arte in the Castello Sforzesco, Milan.*
Laid out in a similar arrangement to the Madonna della Vittoria *which comes from the same period, this work comes from the church of Santa Maria in Organo, in Verona,*

and later passed into the Trivulzio collection. Its original position high over the altar justifies the foreshortening of the saints, who look down towards the viewer. Here, too, the composition is framed within luxuriant vegetation, a further development of the themes learnt in Squarcione's workshop.

34

34, 35. Madonna della Vittoria, *1495–1496, tempera on canvas, 280 × 160 cm. Louvre, Paris. This triumphal composition was commissioned by the Gonzagas* *to celebrate the illusory victory in the battle against the French at Fornovo. The vegetable architecture surrounding the group of figures is spectacular, creating the effect of a garden* *scene, with a pergola, festoons, and the enormous branched piece of coral hanging in the middle.*

36. Parnassus, *1497, canvas, 160 × 192 cm. Louvre, Paris. This is the first of the paintings commissioned by Isabella d'Este, marchesa of Mantua, to decorate her studio. The iconographic scheme, laid down by the court scholar, Paride Ceresara, was especially congenial to Mantegna, who was given scope for his taste for antiquity and mythology, expressed in terms of a cultivated humanism. In the centre, the nine Muses dance to the lyre played by Apollo, while on the right the god Mercury leads forward the winged horse Pegasus; on the rise behind the Muses, Venus and Mars embrace, while Cupid mocks Vulcan, the husband of Venus, in his smithy.*

37. Pallas Expelling the Vices from the Garden of the Virtue, *1504, tempera on canvas, 160 × 192 cm. Louvre, Paris.*
One of Mantegna's last works, completed only two years before his death, and like the **Parnassus,** *intended for the studio of Isabella d'Este. Even richer in literary and moral allusions, this great scene represents the energetic advance of Athene, the goddess of wisdom, in the Garden of the Virtues, from which she is expelling a small crowd of monsters, each representing a single vice. Humanized trees and animated clouds make the scene even more magical and intriguing.*

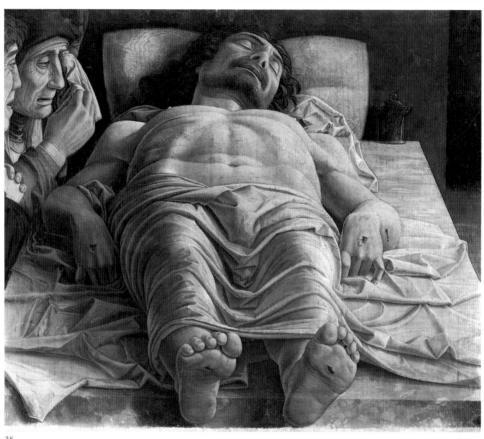

38

38. Dead Christ, c. 1500,
tempera on cavas, 66 × 81 cm.
Pinacoteca di Brera, Milan.
Difficult to date, this canvas is
usually regarded as a late work,
and is included in the inventory
of household goods drawn up by
Mantegna's son after his father's
death. It was intended to
be placed at the foot of his
sepulchre in the chapel he
had built in the church of
Sant'Andrea in Mantua.
In the gloomy light of a cell
in an obitorium, Mantegna
presents the body of Christ,
greyish in colour, reduced
to essentials, placed in rigid
perspective. The Madonna and
other mourners keep watch over
it, like tragic masks emerging
from the shadows on the left.

Anthology of Comments

Your Lordship decorated a chamber so beautiful that truly everyone from this town is talking about it. All who have seen it say that is the most beautiful room in the world. (Zaccaria Saggia da Pisa, Letter to *marchese* Ludovico II Gonzaga, 25 November 1475)

Never did man take up the brush / Or work in other manner / With greater truth than he / Who was the famed heir to antiquity / Nor—without exaggerating— did any / Surpass all of olden times with so much beauty; / For which reason I place him before all others. (G. Santi, *Cronaca Rimata*, begun in 1482)

Andrea always believed that the fine statues of antiquity were more perfect and had more beauties than real bodies; considering that those excellent masters, according to his opinion and judgement, had taken for those statues the whole perfection of nature from many living people, and these perfections rarely come together and are united in a single body, so that it is necessary to take a part from one and another part from another: and in addition to this he believed that statues were more accomplished, and with more details of muscles, veins, nerves, and other particulars, while a natural body, in which the tenderness and softness of the flesh covers over certain harshness, often proves less revealing... and he was known to be very deeply convinced of this opinion when producing his works; in which his manner appears somewhat too incisive, and tends at times towards stone rather than the living flesh.

(G. Vasari, *Le vite de' più eccellenti pittori...*, 1568)

Mantegna was the first in this art [perspective] that opened our eyes for us, for he understood that without this the art of painting is nothing. Hence he has showed us how to make everything correspond to the way we see things; as appears in his works, wrought with great diligence. (G. P. Lomazzo, *Idea del tempio della pittura*, 1590)

In the church of the Eremitani I saw certain paintings by Mantegna, one of the earliest artists, which filled me with wonder. What precise, confident spontaneity in these paintings! From the consideration of this reality, so authentic and not merely superficial, certainly concerned with effect and inspiring fantasies, but also severe, pure, full, earnest, delicate and precise, which had once been tinged with something rigid, studied, awkward, perhaps, later artists learned, as I saw in the paintings of Titian. And only in this way did the vitality of their talent, the strength of their nature, illuminated by the spirit of their predecessors, animated by their strength, grow able to strive ever higher, almost raising themselves above an earthly level, to produce creations that are divine and yet at the same time true. (W. Goethe, *Italienische Reise*, 1786)

Every head [in the *Madonna della Vittoria*] is exemplary in its vividness and character, and some also for their imitation of antiquity. The handling, both in the nudes and in the clothed figures, has a mellowness that refutes the common opinion that Mantegna's style is "dry." Then there is an impasto of colours, a delicacy of brushwork, and a grace all his own, that I feel marks the last step taken by art before achieving the perfection attained by Leonardo. (L. Lanzi, *Storia pittorica dell'Italia*, 1796)

Antiquity was to Mantegna a very different affair, both from what it was to his artist contemporaries in Florence, and from what it is to us now. If ever there be a just occasion for applying the word "Romantic"—and it means, I take it, a longing for a state of things based not upon facts but upon the evocations of art and literature— then that word should be applied to Mantegna's attitude toward antiquity. (B. Berenson, *North Italian Painters of the Renaissance*, 1897)

However fantastic it may seem, I really believe that everything that happened between Padua, Ferrara and Venice between 1450 and 1470—from the most ferocious craziness of Tura and Crivelli to the sorrowful elegance of the young Giambellino and the seemingly rigorous grammar of Mantegna— stemmed from that band of desperate vagabonds, the offspring of tailors, barbers, cobblers and peasants, that passed through Squarcione's workshop over a period of twenty years. A workshop that defies description... where headless classical busts supported spiral frames for triptyches commissioned by the bishops of the Polesine; Florentine plaquettes served as trays for the azure onyxes of Alemannia; Chinese rugs, fierce with monsters, lay alongside moth-eaten bolts of cloth thrown down by Squarcione, "sartor et recamator"; and some trifle from the west miraculously juxtaposed to a Tuscan isometrical view, or a device with armorial bearings painted for some country gentleman. Here and there tawny powder is scattered on the milky plaster of Paris, while all day long Donatello's helpers call in and deliver their turbulent, ironical comments. Here Mantegna grew up alongside the other pupils of Squarcione, and there must have been great debates over what to make of the art of those Florentines, who seemed to fashion clay with the same easy confidence with which God Himself had made man. (R. Longhi, "Lettera pittorica a Giuseppe Fiocco," in *Vita Artistica*, 1926)

Mantegna's personality was complex, in some ways even disturbing; and perhaps by his very greatness, he defies a coherent definition. If, then, he was no humanist, was he a realist? Some might say he was, citing certain unflinching representations, such as the *Dead Christ* in the Brera, the engravings of pagan subjects, or the craggy backgrounds typical of his handling of landscape. But on looking closer, we realize that in this field, for all his remarkable scrutiny of nature—even in the *Madonna of the Caves*, where we find glimmering marble, or in other paintings in which we find irregular paving, as in the *Crucifixion* in the Louvre, and limestone sills with strata of stone and detritus, even when he exalts the texture of matter with an almost geological appropriateness—Mantegna, raising up his dolomitic towers, expresses an unrestrained imagination, related to the effectiveness of the presence of his stony backdrops, closely connected with his adamantine figures. And it is this inclination that led him, after his journey to Rome, to use walls of the tufa or lava peculiar to Lazio in the scenery of his monochromes. He felt their picturesque variety enlivened his systematic compositions. So, after careful study, one realizes that his finest sacred compositions, tending so markedly toward solemnity, are rich in humanity, as if veined with unshed tears, held back with a sublime effort. And this humanity is not realism, but an exquisite and sorrowful feeling for sentiment. (G. Fiocco, *Andrea Mantegna*, 1937)

Despite his abstruse symbolism, which has aroused conflicting opinions in commentators, [the *Parnassus*] is one of the most fresh and appealing works that Mantegna created in this period. Whatever the symbolic significance of the scene, it is poetically valid in musical feeling for rhythm and proportion that links the figures to each other in the serene sweetness of the landscape. This is the last of the artist's classical dreams, inspired by an aesthetic that already anticipates Raphael; an ideal Olympian vision of beauty, in which light and colour take on a leading role, presaging the chromatic relations in the painting of the early Cinquecento. (G. Paccagnini, *Andrea Mantegna*, exhibition catalogue, Palazzo Ducale, Mantua 1961)

Everything—marble, brick, paper and flesh—solidifies into the sumptuousness of a single material, harder and more compact than diamond, gravely crystalising into a gem-like fixity. To achieve this uncompromising effect, the agate hills, the mineralized vegetables, the stony bodies are set in a space created with perpective rigour and of a clarity (there is no trace of air) that seems filtered through lucid crystals that make everything remote. It is this dominion, rationally and constantly exerted by the painter, that imposes his world, so far outside life and time. This is not to deny Mantegna's openness to the beauties of the natural world, the tenderness of motherhood or the charm of children, the elegant vigour of a horse or the friendly liveliness of a dog, or even the varied nature of daily life among the burghers; but each item is set with astounding coherence within the density of lapidary, immutable forms where emotions, nostalgia, disquiet, agressiveness or the fury of pride are placated in controlled harmonies.
(E. Camesasca, Mantegna, 1964)

Mantegna himself seems to have been responsible for placing the altarpiece fittingly in the choir of San Zeno by contributing to the renovation of the presbytery and placing a window on the right to enhance the lighting used in the painting by a source of natural light. He also conceived the frame, so important in the effect of the composition as a whole, in fact the true pivot of the setting created for the painting, through the explicit function of the four semifrontal columns. The tripartite division of the scene they impose is merely apparent (and it is really a misnomer to call this a "triptych"). The columns become identified with the elements of the loggia open to the sky on all sides. The result is that our sense of space does not end in the central ceilinged hall, but extends into an outer quadrilateral, becoming identified with a portion of the single atmospheric belt surrounding the "inhabitated" structure—firm, clear, aseptic atmosphere, from which human respiration is banished—which also includes the zone of air reserved for the viewer, who is automatically transported into the isolation of a surreal experience.
(F. Zava Boccazzi, Mantegna, 1966)

Who was Mantegna in fact? Not even the critics have succeeded in deducing it precisely from their studies of his work. Even the contradictions—above all the contradictions—contribute to his genius; and it is not surprising that Mantegna was regarded by some as "possessed," "disagreeable," "proud and fastidious," and by others as "very gentle," "an incomparable friend," "of amiable manners." In reality the documents show him to have been both gentle and irascible, as are many on earth. Normally chaste (no gossip has come down about him, as it would have had it ever existed), he possessed even a tinge of moralistic austerity unusual amid the loose manners of the Renaissance, and he was quick to accuse others of depraved actions. The constraints of his youth, forcing him into self-love as a defence to save his vocation, his passion for rationalizing his every act, the effort of exerting his imagination and penetrating into his own images, had left a residue of anger in him, which he used to vent in great, ambiguous streams of choler.
(M. Bellonci, Introduction to L'opera completa di Andrea Mantegna, edited by N. Garavaglia, 1967)

As is typical of Mantegna's poetic, here too [in the Dead Christ in the Brera gallery], the simple narrow framing of the scene and the perspective angle amounts to the architectural definition of an interior: a low, grim chamber, the refrigerator cell in a morgue. Looking in on this scene you discover an almost monstruous sight: a heavy body, as if swollen by the disproportion of the almost irreverent perspective angle, with thrust into the foreground two enormous feet pierced through; by its flank appear weeping, grief-stricken masks. But if one looks more intently, one perceives everything in the dim light and the initial emotion is dispelled and replaced by a light of reason, however shaken. One sees another face, like the others creased by numerous ancient lines, which match the dissolving quivering of the watered satin of the pale-rose pillow, the pallid grain of the marble slab, with the onyx veining of the censer, the soaked creases in the shroud that amplify the wounds of the taut, chapped flesh of the wounds, dry as parchment; the wild undulations of the long hair. It is precisely this kind of overwhelming assertion of things that creates the ineluctable sense of the fact of death...

Mantegna's feelings, beyond the apparent coldness—or rather gelidness—of the painting, beyond the emphatic detachment, are the prerogatives of the historian, who, as his calling demands (and above all greatness in his calling), needs to possess great humanity. They are a tragic sense of history and the destiny of man, a blank solitude before his problems which are the same as ever throughout history, the problems of good and evil, of life and death, of happiness and sorrow, universal problems. And at the same time they are feelings of humanity, of faith in the awareness of the spirit which is for everyone, which animates everything, which makes everything rational and comprehensible.
(G.L. Mellini, in *La Pinacoteca di Brera*, 1970)

Mantegna's precocious genius enabled him to work fruitfully in so many different directions at once, and so energetically that it is now hard to tell what he took from one master or another. Certainly he hoarded up everything he was able to assimilate in those fortunate early years; then organized it all in the rigorous framework of "perpectiva artificialis," meditating on this technique until he achieved such mastery of it that he was able to achieve things that the Florentines had never dreamt of doing.
(L. Grossato, *Da Giotto a Mantegna*, exhibition catalogue, Palazzo della Regione, Padua 1974)

Following the rediscovery of the Sala di Pisanello, it is possible to see that Mantegna must also have observed the late Gothic artist's work

carefully, since he used certain ideas from it in the cycle of the Camera degli Sposi. Here I am not referring only to certain bizarre details, like the negro and the dwarf in Pisanello's work, echoed in the negress in the *tondo* and the dwarf mentioned above. Nor do I mean only the arrangement from right to left, which is evident in Pisanello's room, at least in the series of knights errant. Nor do I feel that these brief comments can be limited to mentioning the possible influence of the Tuscan artist in the handling of bifocal perspective and mural technique. Above all, the influence of Pisanello on Mantegna appears in the overall and unified organization of the chamber decorated.
(E. Marani, in *I Gonzaga a Mantova*, 1975)

The illusionistic values reach their summit [in the *Camera degli Sposi*], a level never attained again, or at least one that Mantegna never pursued with a coherent perspective system... These illusionistic values are, however, a feature of all his work and appear even in his early years, when he was trained in a Padua permeated with experiments in perspective... The originality of Mantegna's use of perspective lies in his interpretation of Tuscan perspective, which he always subordinated to expressive, dramatic or lyrical aims, involving the spectator through a hypnotic perspective-illusionistic apparatus. His conception of space is closely bound up with the setting for which each work was intended and the subject represented, as well as directly related to the movements of the viewer. Mantegna's work certainly

heralds the illusionistic experiments of later centuries.
(C. Badini, *Mantegna e la prospettiva*, exhibition catalogue, Casa del Mantegna, Mantua 1983)

Without underrating the particular nature of the education he received from Francesco Squarcione, it appears that Andrea also learnt a great deal from his early Venetian experiences, through the study of not only Jacopo Bellini but also Antonio Vivarini and Giovanni d'Alemagna, and through the study of the traditions of religious iconography in Venice. As with Donatello, he certainly rejected many things; in fact it can be said that the flowery late-Gothic manner still usual in the Venetian workshops could hardly have held much interest for a young artist already intent upon reviving the ideal perfection of ancient painting. All the same, it would be an error to underestimate the effect of these other factors on Mantegna's art: even in the perfection of his paintings these influences remain perceptible, since—apart from his grandiose leanings towards modernity and the ancient world — Mantegna, like all of the artists and art patrons of his time, had composite cultural origins.
(R. Lightbown, *Mantegna*, 1986)

The San Zeno altarpiece is Mantegna's most mature achievement in terms of the experiments he had conducted, from his very earliest works, into the illusory representation of real space in relation to the point of view of the viewer; and it has a number of points of contact with the two

Stories of Saint Christopher painted for the Erimitani both in terms of the lucid perspective code, based at San Zeno on the principle of a lowered point of view, with the painter presenting a unified space beyond the pciture frame in which the *Sacra Conversazione* takes place, and also in terms of the decorative and antiquarian features.
(A. De Nicolò Salmazo, in *La pittura nel Veneto. Il Quattrocento*, 1990)

The most remarkable innovation in Mantegna's wall paintings in Mantua is the use of light, the real light falling from the windows and the slanted light within the painting, used to enhance and reveal. In a certain sense Mantegna had no choice in the matter: the extensive presence of false reliefs in the vaulting called for an unambiguous and coordinated definition of the sources of light to illuminate them. But in the *Camera degli Sposi* there is a new capacity of light to bathe and reveal the colouring, which is certainly still defined by a solid linear framework that goes back to Donatello, Filippo Lippi and Andrea del Castagno, capable of modulating a position in space, as is shown by the way colour and light are used to define the so-called "nurse" to the left of the mantelpiece, through variations of shades of white, grey and black. It is the experience of Flemish painting that Mantegna reveals, and not just in technical terms, together with the *luminismo* of Piero della Francesca. The varied complexity he is capable of presenting with precise clarity and studied decorum explains the importance his contemporaries saw in Man-

tegna's painted ornaments and the constant interest and attention he evoked throughout the Renaissance, which he anticipated and expressed to perfection.
(M. Cordaro, *La Camera degli Sposi*, 1992)

To trace Mantegna's career is to participate in the transformation of the youth who painted the frescoes in the Ovetari Chapel in Padua with their romantic evocation of Roman monuments and buildings; to the dedicated student of ancient literature and archaeology who conceived the Imperial Roman temple in the *Circumcision* [Plate 12], embellished with coloured marbles and gilt bronze ornament, and adorned the vault of the Camera Picta with feigned marble busts of the Caesars set against a pseudo-mosaic background; to the reincarnation of those ancient masters whose works, long since lost, had been held up to him as paradigms.
(K. Christiansen, "The Art of Andrea Mantegna," in *Mantegna*, exhibition catalogue, Royal Academy of Arts, London 1992)

Paradoxically, it was only at the end of his life that Mantegna's paintings seem to illustrate specifically some of the subjects Alberti promoted in *De Pictura*, written over seventy years earlier. By that time they were out of date by the standards of Leonardo, Michelangelo and Raphael. The *Pallas Expelling the Vices* [Plate 37] is peopled with allegorical personifications, each betraying its character through gesture and facial expression, reinforced by inscriptions which, according to

Alberti, would place the painter on a par with the writer. And a drawing, which may be the last by his hand to survive, or the *Calumny of Apelles* illustrates the best-known example of a "historia," for Alberti, the highest form of painting.
(L. Gowing, "Mantegna," in *Mantegna*, exhibition catalogue, Royal Academy of Arts, London 1992)

Such reflections tell us something of the grave import and the personal meaning which we feel in the fixity of Mantegna's style itself. It is there, at the centre of his art, in the very character of the figuration, whose force is so close to self-annihilation that we feel a quality of the sublime. It has the consistency of a deadly passion, a passion which the sensuous surface of the arts rarely admits, but one that is deep within us nonetheless. This is the context that gives to Mantegna's moments of tenderness their special and unique significance. In his little Madonna pictures, Mother and Child are drawn together more profoundly than in any others. The mother enfolds the child, as if to contain him; a single contour encloses the two in a monolithic block. It is a truer view of natural tenderness, truer in its implicit recognition of the natural forces that beset it—than any but the very greatest of the humane painters have shown. The intimate truth of it is perhaps the explanation of the unexpected link between Mantegna and Rembrandt.
(D. Chambers, J. Martineau, R. Signorini, "Mantegna and the Men of Letters," in *Mantegna*, exhibition catalogue, Royal Academy of Arts, London 1992)

Essential Bibliography

Andrea Mantegna, exhibition catalogue edited by G. Paccagnini, Palazzo Ducale, Mantua 1961.

G. Paccagnini, *Andrea Mantegna*, Milan 1961.

R. Cipriani, *Tutta la pittura del Mantegna*, Milan 1962.

E. Camesasca, *Mantegna*, Milan 1964.

F. Zava Boccazzi, *Mantegna*, Florence 1966.

N. Garavaglia, *L'opera completa di Andrea Mantegna*, Milan 1967.

Da Giotto al Mantegna, exhibition catalogue edited by L. Grossato, Palazzo della Ragione, Padua, 1974.

G. Amadei, E. Marani, *I Gonzaga a Mantova*, Milan 1975.

A. Sartori, *Documenti per la storia dell'arte a Padova*, Vicenza 1976.

A. Martindale, *The Triumphs of Caesar*, London 1979.

Splendours of the Gonzaga, exhibition catalogue, Victoria and Albert Museum, London, 1981.

Mantegna e la prospettiva, exhibition catalogue edited by C. Badini, Casa del Mantegna, Mantua, 1988.

R. Lightbown, *Mantegna*, London 1986.

Mantegna, exhibition catalogue edited by J. Martineau, Royal Academy of Arts, London 1992.